Fuck It,

Smile Anyway

By: Allysia Altick

Table of Contents

4- Art Class Assignment
5- Water
6- Never Ending Battles
7- Start Again
8- Home?
9- Dear Hamlet
10- The face of Ophelia
11- Ophelia
12- Lady Macbeth
13- Juliet
14- Utter Peace
15- Violet Butterflies
16- Meet Again
17- Young Girls
18- Follow Joy
19- Thunderstorms
20- Portals
21- Serenity
22- Time
23- Color in Life
24- Acceptance
25- The Stars are Always Young
26- Clarity
27- Distance
28- To Die Today
29- Innocence and Berries
30- Wonderland
31- Deception
32- Battlefield
33- Tire Swing
34- Cliche
35- Devin

36- Circles
37- Strength
38- Tonight
39- Wind
40- Hidden by the Night
41- Feel
42- Hope
43- Dreaming or Drowning
44- When You're Gone
45- Invisible Tears
46- Cope
47- A Little More
48- Beautiful
49- Move On
50- For the Moment
51- The Mask
52- Exposed
53- Head Start
54- I am Me
55- Dear Flower
56- I missed you
57- Carry On
58- Wounded wing
59- Nothing to say
60- Wait on you
61- Together but Apart
62- The Score
63- A Man?
64- No Longer

Art Class Assignment
Create a Piece and Write some Lines Describing an Emotion
~~My Feeling is Magical~~

My feeling is Magical. This picture relates to me because I always try to find the Magic in things. No matter what is going on something else is happening on a deeper level. I can see the Magic in Love between families and men and women everyday. I love sitting out on a dock at night watching all the lights reflect and dance off the water. It makes me smile seeing the smile on a child's face when he sees his favorite teddy bear.

I watch peoples faces, taking in the emotions that dance across their features. All the while they are unaware of the picture they are painting in my mind.

Magic is created by your heart and you have to choose to see the beauty in ordinary things. You would never know the mysterious sounds at night soothed you until they were gone. Magic is a secret garden, a blazing sunset, a soft teddy bear, an old wood swing and colorful rainbows. It is looking for the deeper meaning in life. The feelings that make the bad ones worth while.

Water

I am like water
   Always moving
Sometimes a little
   Restless
Still forever
   Winding towards
Another paradise
   Always
   Returning
   Home

Never Ending Battles

Plan A
Plan B
All the way through Z

Fight the great fight
Gather all of your might
Follow the path

That You gave You
Do all you can do
Then do more

Start Again

Hello, Goodbye, Sigh, Cry
Wake up and move
Brush your hair, Smooth
Clear your eyes

You're not allowed to cry
You tried
Fight harder, Smarter
Your thoughts, Gather

This is not the End
No, it's not pretend
Look yourself in the face
Start Again

Home?

What to expect?
Where to go?
How do I truly know?

Where my life should be
Where I can be free

From doubt and harm
Somewhere with loving arms
Just a shelter under the stars

Anywhere will do
As long as it is with you

This train of thought
Taunts me a lot

Because my home
Just may be you

Dear Hamlet

Down by the river

I ease my heart

Washing the unsolvable away

I descend myself

Into the clear depths

Where lies are transparent

The Face of Ophelia

Eyes wide in naive innocence

With lips to kiss the truth

Grace in the posture of a martyr

Whose face speaks of the wild

Cruelness disposed from heart

To the wild tangles

Banished to the place unseen

by the angel that wears them

Ophelia

Innocence corrupts the mind

Vulnerability to love and pain

Only brings death in

Slowly drifting rain

Rosemary to remember you

Rue to those who will weep

For the young ending on the sheet

Lady Macbeth

Unknown words slip off my tongue
Of hands unclean
From damage I have done

Witchcraft consoles me
As my lover will become
The king of all others
Under the sun

A nose of deception
A mouth full of greed
To my death, my faults lead me and mine

My hair being as black
As my soul
Corruption has sent me
Out of control

Juliet

Eyes closed

To the violent vengeance

Puckered lips

For my banished love

Locks as straight

As the innocence

That shines through

Utter Peace

Crystal dew on grass and a sunset ablaze
A weary midnight dream to get through the summer days
Sitting on a porch swing in the early morn
Cuddling with a loved one
When you are already warm

Seasons pass by slowly
While endless breezes fly by
If I had to say goodbye now
I would be okay to fly
On the wings of my love
Into the endless sky above

I would give my last breath today
I would die in peace
Only this way

Violet Butterflies

Violet butterflies are attracted by tears

They fly around you

They carry away your fears

All while whispering soft lullabies

The surround and invade your heart

They hold you together

While you're falling apart

They will not ask your deepest secrets

They cannot lie

Their purpose is to comfort

These magical little flying things
Will not bring you shiny rings
But they can give you what you need
A secret friend

Meet Again

As soon as happy days begin

True love finds true life's end

Lovers finding peace in life

Savoring ones held dear

Love comes in different

Forms and although

Lovers may mourn

It will not be best to

Become bitter and forget

All the love surrounding you

Until you meet again

Young Girls

Joyous Songs

Endless breeze

Bright Light Shining

Through Swaying Trees

Quiet Footsteps

On an Old Dirt Road

Loving Thoughts

Come into the World

Through a Serene Tune

Of a Young Girls Heart

Follow Joy

As time moves on

You need to be quick

But also be careful

The road is slick

The road of life

Has bumps and curves

Street lights broken

Keep on going

No matter how rough

You've got to be strong

Going through hard times

Just follow the sound

Of joyous wind chimes

Thunderstorms

Lovely sights

Walking through

Endless midnight

Comforting breaths

Of a sweet

Thunderstorm breeze

Puts my mind

At rest

And pain

At ease

Portals

A portal like a looking glass

A window into one souls past

Hidden secrets

A sought after prize

The place where true beauty lies

Is on display in your eyes

Serenity

S ouls that are searching

E verywhere, all the time

R eady to be loved and believe

E veryone has the right

N ot to worry so much

I ntroduced to peace

T aking it all in and hoping that

Y earning is no longer present

Time

Time goes by slow
Sometimes too fast
You have to hold on
Make what you have, last

Love with the trust
That they'll never leave
Never betray the part of you
That only you can see

Laugh not with the least concern of
What will happen tomorrow
The warmth in your heart
Radiate it with your voice

Color in Life

A pen is black

A boring dull way to bring a page to life

No eyes have to behold

But still,.

Within the black

A story is told

No need to enhance your "hype"

Live Life in Color

Because,…

There is always Color in Life

Acceptance

If I die today
I know I will leave
On the wings of the
Kindest butterfly
So that I may be flown
To my next home
My last one glowing below

If I die today
I ask that you not cry
For the love
I feel for you

Will be displayed
In the sky

The Stars are Always Young

Stormy nights and a
Velvet breeze
Throwing rocks at
Old oak trees

Honeysuckle on my tongue
Never forgetting
That you're young

Warmth of heart
In a young love
Sending wishes to
Shooting stars above

Clarity

In this moment

My mind is still

My heart is full

I've lost my will

To worry about the future

For the present is too great

To taint these memories

With the struggles

Of the Day to Day

Distance

Wherever you travel
No matter how far
Remember, I'm where you are

I give you this flower
This rose resembles my love
The journeys I've been through
To receive you ,my love

The tears I've shed
Have hardened this stem
The pain I've felt has made this rose red

But the joy I have felt
Has made this flower bloom
This is my love
I give it to you

To Die Today

To die today

That would be a crime

A serene chaos inside my soul

Does not define

The words I speak are mime

The grass grows blind

The truth will not sound

Until the sun is found

So darken the sky

Let feeling fly

To die on a cloudy day

That would be a crime

Innocence and Berries

Silly dreams

Creating scenes

In my head

While I lay in my

Make shift bed

By my eyes unseen

A place too mean

Fallen oak used as a chair

Swimming naked

With uncombed hair

Caring not of the hardships

Imposed on you by becoming a man

Innocence tastes like wild berries

WONDERLAND

W inding down a narrow road

O nly thing in sight is

N ever ending trees and flowers hiding creatures that have been

D ancing for hours

E verybody filled with glee

R edheads, green faces, purple eyes

L aughing loudly

A ll is well and being well is for all

N ot a tear of sadness, They're

D enied a place to fall

Deception

You've got problems

Trouble is,.. we are just alike

Laughing at the anger

Secrets hidden in the night

Biding our time

Committing subtle attempts

To get in each others head

Broke into each others

Heart instead

Battlefield

I am lifted by sturdy boards

That were put here to hold

Entertainers of all kinds

For audiences to behold

The lights I cannot see now

But I know they are there

They give glory and fame

To all who dare

To put their hearts and souls

Out on the line

For people to judge

This stage is a battlefield

Id like to see you

Try and be one of us

Tire Swing

I feel one thing beneath me

Not dirt nor grass

It sways and swirls freely

Climbing higher

With my spirits

My mind roams free

Heart soaring above

The hate of those

Who deny they hear me

I speak the truth though

It only matters to me

So I swing

To fly and feel free

Cliche

How do I love thee? Let me count the ways
I love your gentle walk and how your brown hair sways
You are a beauty and you love me!
Oh how I burn with glee!

But now what comes our way?
A handsome looking man seeming rather gay
He takes your hand and asks you to dance
And I can see from your sideways glance

I have no fear for our love conquers all
Even that stupid man, however tall
All is fair in love and war
Ahhh, He beat me

Well, better to have loved and lost than to never have loved at all
O'wait beautiful blonde maiden
Do you believe in love at first sight?

Devin

Sunshine landing on my face
After a long journey home
From the land of wild dreams
Where all hearts aren't made of stone
Where beauty lies in every heart
Joy lay in their eyes

So I ask the sunshine why?
Why trek back to a place
Where hearts are filled with lies
Where the only thing you see in eyes
Is the solemn lonely need to cry

The sunshine fills my soul
It gives me hope to make it
Through these days
And now I know

Happiness is a question

The answer,
Lies in you

Circles

Spinning, flying in a

drizzling gray sky

Looking down on a

green and blue sea

Smiling, suddenly

filled with glee

You notice the absence

of dreary thoughts

Fall back

Into the water

Drown in a sea

of depression

Lost love and

Untouched dreams

Strength

Sometimes I feel like I'm in a tale
Like I cannot escape, like I cannot prevail
I want to go home, I want to see the light
To know what it feels to be far beyond fright

I feel so blind, only numbness and pain
Yet I travel so far and I'm still without gain
I hope the numb never fades
And the pain go away

So that one day
 I can find the strength to stay
The pain I suffer day after day
Sometimes I wish I could just walk away

Burning in pain
lost in fear
Its a wonder how
I'm still thinking clear

The good times we had
The memories we share
But your eyes I can't see
you're no longer here

I may not see you
For a very long time
I don't know what I'll do
To waste that time

Tonight

I see you
But you don't see me
That's When I knew
It could never be
I gave you my heart
You ripped it in two
Played with it
Until it was through
Then finally
When I had to take it back
I felt so hurt
But not you
Why should I say
What you already know
That I cant walk away
I cant let you go
So tonight I wanna cry
To let you go
To say goodbye

Wind

When your life fades into shades of gray and lonely greens.

Love is hidden in a vibrant garden that hasn't bloomed.

You need to keep going until you find out why.

Why the wind picks up everything you care about?

Why does it blow it away?

Lost to the breeze.

Now you are locked in a secret garden.

Its dying.

A dying garden hidden by the wind.

Hidden by the Night

Nobody knows all the thoughts

Running through my head

Or all of the tears

That have landed on my bed

Or how I cry most every night

Wake up and lie to myself

Say everything's alright

No one knows about my dreams

They only know how I seem to be

And I always seem to be alright

My feelings are hidden by the night

Feel

Not done but still going
How is it clear to see
All of these the that happen around me
How in the world did I end up here
So cold and alone with absence of cheer
I see laughter, joy and friendship too
But feel nothing all the way through
Not a tear of sadness or a hint of joy
I show no emotion
Like a baby doll toy
I want to speak the truth
But too cold it seems
As I try to hold on
However hard it may be
I walk through that door
With pride in my hand
But my heart is missing
On a far away land
Numb all over yet the tears still fall
How after all this did I lose my control
I failed the test but walked the straight line
Its still unbelievable, leaving me mime
At the end of this
My eyes cant see
My heads filled with anger
Letting the feelings free

HOPE

When will rainy days cease to begin?

When will sunny days never have an end?

I think the rain
Reminds me…

That even after the storms of life.

The sun will always peek through

The despaired clouds

And shine new light

Into my hurting heart

Dreaming or Drowning

Drowning in tragic pain and sorrow
My love is hidden at the bottom
Of a beautiful blooming ocean

As my heart sinks lower
Deep purple aquatic flowers
Take root beneath me
Pushing dreams back into my reach

As the dreams make their way back
My thoughts float back to light
Bringing the flowers with them

But the flower dies
As I break the surface

I don't know which is worse
Dreaming or Drowning

When You're Gone

When you're gone
The minutes pass so slowly
I want to feel your warmth
I want to hear your voice
But I also want to know
That I'm making my choice

In my mind
I don't want you here
But in my heart
You leaving is my worst fear

I hope you know that I love you
And somehow you still love me too
I know now why I fight it
I know why I lie
They are my defenses
So that I don't cry

Unlike anyone else
I'm starting to realize
Just what I look like
Through other peoples eyes

I thought strong meant no weakness
I thought no one should see
The times I search for the shadows
And just want to flee

Invisible Tears

Invisible tears

Carry away

All the things

I can't say

They drown my heart

They feed my fear

That one day

You won't be here

No one can see them

Only me..

Until you come

And make me believe

You love me tough

And take a stand

My tears become visible

As you take my hand

Cope

Your eyes are mean
Your heart is cold
You shut your eyes
So not to see me cry

I hate you
You changed on me
You say horrible things now
Does it make you proud?
To turn what we had to demise
Please, Look me in the eyes

I loved you
Maybe still do
To me it was true
I guess not to you

I had to flee
Before you changed me
It was too late
You closed the gate

So now,...
Even when you're gone
I can't be strong
Unless I take to wearing a mask
Too look like we have no past

A Little More

Floating..

Dream like haze

Afraid to open my eyes

Lost and happy

To be somewhere else

I feel..

The cold wet

Seeping into my skin

Clearing my violated mind

With the sound of waves

Hitting the shore

I don't want to go there

Just let me sink

A little more

Please

Beautiful

Beautiful..

Carrying a cold heart

With a somber face

Beautiful eyes

No trust in these depths

Your self duty to deceive and lie

Your lips meet mine

They do not satisfy

The ache in my soul

Only bodily pleasures from you

No ability to let yourself fall

So while you stand tall

I'll walk away

Feeling nothing but sorrow

That you didn't have the strength

To let go of the pain

And fall

Just like the rain

Move On

Giggles whisper through the air
Smile on my face
Hand and hand
Through the sand
Worries gone
I've learned to be strong
No need with you
I can love my past
Forget the bad times
I'll make my peace offering with a rhyme
I've found myself
New love has found me too
I hope it finds you
After all we've been through
I still love you
But in a different sort
I have no harsh words
Left on flying birds
Serenity in my heart
I always feared being apart
Separation from you cut me deep
But now there's him
A healthier love
Not as crazy and wild
Done with the hurt
Forever and always
You're in my heart
So make your life great
Love a woman
Like you too are tired of the hate

For the Moment

Go ahead, Walk away

I'll bite my tongue

Save my words

For another day

Friends are forever

Lies are unbinded

They unwind

They define you

I want you to go

Leave me alone

Friends aren't forever

They're for the moment

The Mask

Carry on they said. Be strong they said. Everyone told me to do what they couldn't. Being strong is a phrase that can be manipulated. They say the word strong like it's the perfect option.

Strong is manipulated until your wearing a mask. A front that traps beholders into thinking you don't care. You're not hurt. It doesn't matter. Nothing happened. You feel no pain. You are Strong

You're not strong. You're fake. I was fake. I fell into that place where being strong meant being someone else. I forgot who and what I felt so I could seem to be strong. I held on for so long. Only to find that I was hindering my ability to move forward.

I choose to leave that mask behind today. Now I live for me. It's the only way.

Exposed

Light is shining through the trees

Kiss me now

When no one sees

Lips are soft

Eyes are closed

With you,

I leave my heart

Exposed

Head Start

Begin on Empty

Fly on a broken wing

Strength today

Gives tomorrow a chance to be

Care only for those

Who deserve your time

Make peace of mind

Before your voice is mime

Happiness survives a state of heart

Let it be

Live life with a

Head start

I am Me

The first day. Sophomore year. Feels brand new. I am me. No one can hurt me.

I know that people still talk. I refuse to listen. I am above their fake lines drawn to stagger lives of innocent people. I loved him. The "ed" doesn't change much in my heart. Everyone, including myself needs to know what is in the past.

The past cannot define me. I define myself by how I interpret the past and carry it into my future. A mask I used to wear now lies on my bedroom floor, for it has served it's purpose. I no longer need to injure my faith and self so I can pride on a front that everyone believes. Except me. I hated the lies and yet they comforted me.

Today, I leave the mask completely.
I am Me.

Dear Flower

Dear flower,
Why do you bloom?
The world too rude
For your beauty
What do you see?
If not the lies,
Be it the love?
Of a mother and child
A woman's scorn
On a humbled man
Walking through an
Uncrowded street
The holding of a hand?
Flower?
Why cry in the morn?
While beasts and pets arise
I'd like to see through your eyes
When the morning dew
Settles in the morn
The same day has
A different change
The beautiful bloom
You produce
Is my world
I want to
Live like a flower

I Missed You

Do not pierce me

In that way

Your gaze

Shreds my heart

Your will

Phases me

You're unaware of

Your guilt

Myself, betrays me

A jumping rhythm

Close to yours

No penalty

Just words

Calm me now

I missed you

But won't admit how much

Carry On

Carry on
The quiet one
Standing alone
Without a shun
With a strong mind
Most will not find
Behind the eyes
That mesmerize
The shallow hearts
Of the careless

Carry on
The creative one
Being yourself
The only one
Your thoughts
Your own
Your life to stretch
Out for people
To catch
Meaning and emotion

Carry on
The shameless one
Your flaws are perfect
Will is done
Own up to mistakes
Know what it takes
To outshine the sun
Blur trespasses into new
Shades of life
Into a brighter hue

Wounded Wings

Carry on..

Climb on my wounded wings

We can fly among the caged bird

Listen to what I am saying

No words

When all hope is gone

Your wounds become mine

My heart ceases to want time

Goodbye

Nothing to Say

Why won't you save me?
I need to be freed
I'm stuck in a hell
That only I can see

You cute me with words
You destroy me over time
You drained me
Of every emotion and dime

So go away
Let this be the last time
Your face
Is so close to mine

You never loved me
How could it be true
Lovers don't just leave
Out of the blue

Lovers love comfort
They always stay
Now to you
I have nothing to say

Wait on You

He does not think

I am Beautiful

These words are never said

Only criticisms from you lips

Our deal not yet unbroken

Unsure you will come through

I'll play my part

I'll wait on you

Together but Apart

Lead me on a wild ride
Careless beginnings
Not only for tonight
Let me feel what I hide

All our doubts
Begin and end with them
Your voice is weak
Unusual for your shout

Because of that our love is bound
Hidden
Not to be found
Love, Together but apart

Carry me on your heart
Never let me down
Forget your pride as I have mine
Let us never be apart

Lost the words that sing
New sensations
Only brave thoughts
Allowed for you to bring

Courageous tones I wan t to sound
Honor in my heart
Caring words that lead to actions
All found, together but apart

The Score

Deep sounds, Deaf heart

Startled words that fall apart

I no longer believe in your mind

I believe all faith is created in time

Still I am bound

Beyond my reach

No matter how often I preach

Of independence forever more

Now it's time to settle the score

A Man?

Do I know what I do?
How about you?
Do you know how one action
Causes a reaction

A reaction causes another action
Maybe these plots
Give you satisfaction

Your brain is quick but
My heart is thicker
You will have to hit harder
To put down this ginger

You aren't a man
You can't even stand alone
So you drag me down

I believed in you
But better sense
Thats the better man
That I've found

No Longer

Forgot to listen
Forgot to care
To all the words
You threw in the air

I hope you're happy
I hope she's rad
I also hope
she's not a fad

You've made your bed
Now here's your shit
Those accusations
Yeah, you can quit

Go away
Have your fun

Just know that
I am no longer
Your home

Made in United States
Orlando, FL
01 September 2022